325
Creative Prompts
for Personal Journals
by J.A. Senn

325
Creative Prompts
for Personal Journals

by J.A. Senn

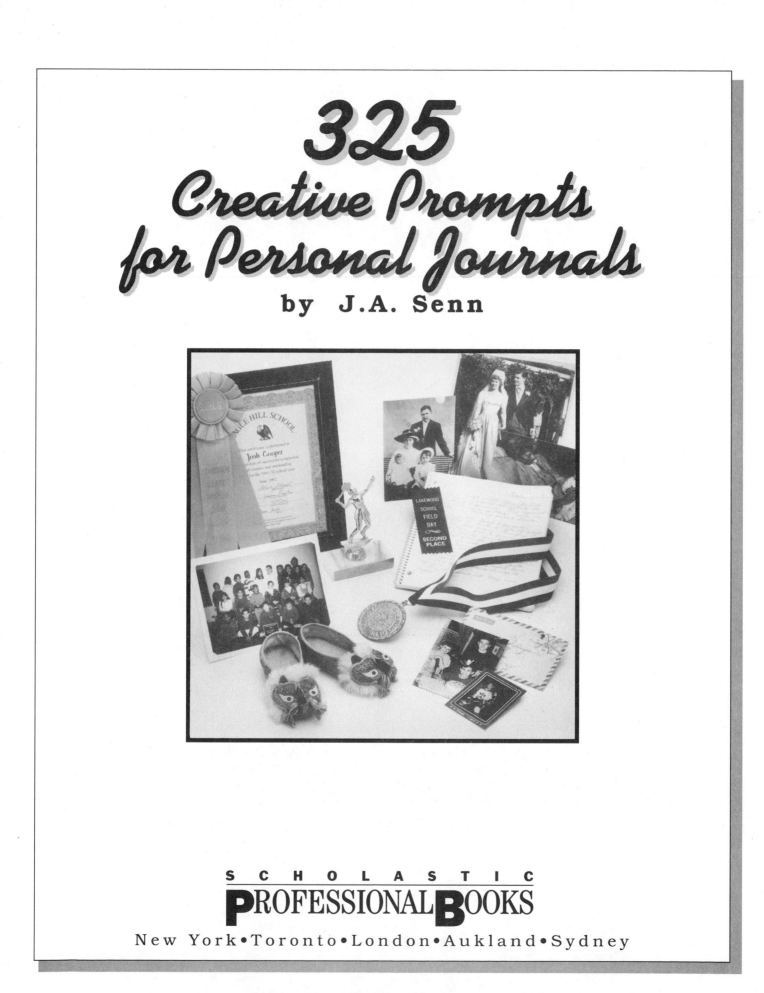

SCHOLASTIC
PROFESSIONAL BOOKS

New York•Toronto•London•Aukland•Sydney

For information regarding permission, write to Scholastic, Inc., 730 Broadway, New York, NY   10003.

Designed by Vincent Ceci
Cover design by Vincent Ceci
Cover photograph by Donnelly Marks
Interior illustration by Mona Mark
ISBN 0-590-49350-7
Copyright © 1992 by J.A. Senn

Table of Contents

Introduction
Page 7

How to Use This Book
Page 9

Chapter 1
Personal Interests and Experiences
Page 13

Chapter 2
Memories
Page 19

Chapter 3
Families and Friends
Page 23

Chapter 4
Current Affairs
Page 27

Chapter 5
School Subjects
Page 31

Chapter 6
Multicultural Connections
Page 35

Chapter 7
Quotations
Page 39

Bibliography
Page 47

Introduction

*L*earning to write can be very much like learning to ride a bicycle. At first, students are wobbly and unsure of themselves, but the more they practice, the better they become. It is this sort of practice that writing in personal journals provides. Not only does journal writing help students to become better writers, but it also provides them a marvelous source of future writing ideas. Along the way, many students also improve their thinking skills and actually develop a genuine enjoyment of writing.

J. A. Senn

How To Use This Book

Getting Started

Basically, students need only a notebook, and most any kind will work. You probably will want to keep the journals of young students in the classroom, but older students should be allowed to take them home occasionally so that their home environment can also be a stimulus for some journal entries.

Most teachers give their students five or ten minutes every day to write in their journals—often early in the day or at the beginning of a class period when their students are still fresh and full of ideas. Then always remind your students to write about whatever is on their minds, or—if they can't think of anything to write about—give them one of the prompts in this book. Just keep in mind that your students should always be writing about themselves—their ideas, thoughts, dreams, and opinions. From time to time, you also may want to remind them of the difference between journals and diaries: People record their actions in diaries, but they record their reactions in journals.

What goes in a journal should be somewhat flexible—according to the ages and abilities of your students. Most teachers encourage their students to express themselves in various forms—including poetry as well as prose. Some students might even draw a picture from time to time instead of writing, or enter the lyrics of a song and then include their reactions to the words. Almost anything can be included in a journal—if it reflects some thought or idea of the writer.

All journal entries should, of course, be dated, and many teachers have their students write in pen because it is more permanent, and makes their entries easier to read later on. Writing with a pen should also reinforce the fact that you will not correct their journal entries for errors in spelling and grammar. Lifting this pressure from your students should give them the confidence necessary to fully explore their thoughts and ideas and to express themselves freely.

After your students have written in their journals for several weeks or months, be sure to have them go into their journals to find a topic for a specific writing assignment. Such an activity will reinforce one of the valuable fringe benefits of journal writing: interesting topics to write about—right at their fingertips. Gone forever will be the unrelenting cry,

"I don't have anything to write about!" Your students will soon find out that they not only can find many wonderful ideas to write about in their journals, but they will also soon discover that when they write about topics that interest them, their end results are much better.

Protecting Your Students' Right to Privacy

As students are writing in their journals, some teachers go around the classroom, reading over their students' shoulders and writing notes on the sides of various journal pages. These notes, usually in response to something students have written, can help students think more deeply about a certain subject or topic. In their next journal entry, some students will then respond to the teacher's comments. Although there are many positive benefits to this interactive approach, there is one potential problem: students may restrict what they write because they don't want their teacher reading anything too personal. To avoid this problem—and to protect your students' right to privacy—you could tell your students that you will only comment on certain days, or that they should cover their writing if they don't want you to read it.

Evaluating Journals

On the other hand, if you never look at your students' journals or evaluate them in any way, many students will simply not write faithfully in their journals—or at least, not take this activity seriously. Therefore, some form of teacher response is usually necessary, but you should always avoid any actual grading of the journal entries themselves. Too often with formal writing assignments, students get discouraged when they get back a piece of their writing with lots of red marks on it. They often conclude that, indeed, they can't write because they always make so many "mistakes."

If you do not correct your students' journals, how, then, can you evaluate them? Teachers across the country have come up with the following suggestions and ideas

- Observe students each day as they write in their journals.
- At the end of each week, month, or quarter, have students submit a "portfolio" of from one to five of their favorite journal entries. Then read and evaluate only these. This method also develops students' critical thinking skills as they learn to evaluate which entries they think are best. (If using this method, then a notebook with removeable/replaceable pages, like a ring binder, is best.)
- At the end of each week, month, or quarter, choose different

categories—such as the most unusual entry and/or the funniest entry. Then after students submit just those entries, you can read and evaluate them, but none of the others.
• Have students count the number of entries they have included in a given period of time, and give a mark for nothing more than mere quantity.
• Create evaluation forms that ask students to check various things such as the number of entries, the kinds of entries, and even their favorite entries.
• At least twice a year, have students go into their journals to look for a specific idea to write about.
• For younger students, you may want to read over all of their entries—after you have invited them to take out any personal entries they don't want anyone to read.

The bottom line, however, is that you must do what works best for you and your students by providing enough evaluation to encourage everyone to keep their journals current—without making your students feel that their entries are under too much scrutiny.

Generating Your Own Journal Prompts

Although much journal writing is self-inspired, some teachers have found a need to have a storehouse of prompts to offer their students when they say, "I don't know what to write about. Although this book provides 325 specific ideas to get students writing in their journals, you may still want to develop some of your own from time to time. Following are some suggestions you can use to generate your own journal writing prompts.

1. Begin with a theme. You could use the themes in your reading or literature book, or you could use some general themes such as those that follow below. Once you have chosen a theme, write down everything that comes to your mind about it. This is also a fun activity to do with students, and it usually produces many worthwhile ideas.
   • sports   • pets
   • television   • hobbies
   • family   • school

2. As you flip through any magazine or newspaper, look at the pictures, the titles of the articles, and even the advertisements. Without exception, you will find a variety of ideas for journal prompts. For example, an advertisement for an automobile could lead to any of the following journal writing ideas.

• If you were a car, describe how you would look.

• If you could buy a car for your family, what kind would you choose? Explain your choice.

• How would your life be different if your parents did not own a car?

• If you could invent something new to add to a car, what would it be? Explain your answer.

3. Read the titles in your reading or literature book (and text books in other subject areas) and look at the pictures. Both activities should produce many ideas.

4. Look through a book of quotations and choose some relevant ones.

5. Glance through a card catalog or an encyclopedia to find unusual or timely topics.

6. Think about anything current such as television programs, the season of the year, a special event at the school or in the community, or even the weather.

Using the Prompts in This Book

As you begin to use the journal prompts on the following pages, keep in mind that all of them may not be appropriate for all of your students. Therefore, read over as many as you can in each particular chapter and choose only those that are relevant and/or suitable for your students. Although there is often little to distinguish one prompt from another—according to age or grade level—the entries have been arranged so that those appealing to younger students appear first and those appealing to older students appear at the end of each chapter. However, you probably will find that most of the prompts will work well with students of any age. You also may want to consider reading a prompt aloud to your students—especially your younger students—and then discussing it briefly before having them start to write.

Chapter 1

Personal Interests and Experiences

Many recent studies have produced the same results: students write best when they write about topics that interest them and have some personal relevance to their lives. Surely there are no topics more interesting—or that have any greater relevance—to young people than topics about themselves: their lives, their interests, and their experiences. That's why this chapter about personal interests and experiences is the first and longest. Be sure to add your own ideas to this chapter as well—ideas that give consideration, perhaps, to such things as regional differences. Then over the years, highlight those writing prompts that have worked best with your students.

1.

Explain what you like and dislike about your name.

2.

List the reasons why you would like to be covered with fur like an animal—instead of wearing clothes.

3.

Would you like to be a prince or a princess—instead of yourself? Explain your answer.

4.

What is your favorite holiday? Write the reasons for your choice.

5.

Write freely about your worst fear.

6.

Write about your favorite pet—one you have now or have had in the past. What did it look like? Why did you like it so much? (If you have never had a pet, write about a perfect pet—one you would like to have.)

7.

What do you like and dislike about where you live?

8.

Write freely about the bravest thing you have ever done.

9.

List the things you worry about. Then write about the thing you worry about most.

10.

What is your favorite fairy tale? Write the reasons why you like it so much.

11.

If you could be a superhero, what extraordinary powers would you give yourself? Explain your choices.

12.

What is one of your pet peeves? Explain why it bothers you.

13.

Describe how you look when you make your funniest face. (NOTE: Younger children may first want to draw a picture of their funniest face.)

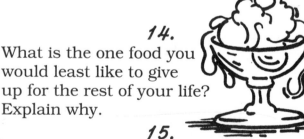

14.

What is the one food you would least like to give up for the rest of your life? Explain why.

15.

What is your favorite color? Write the reasons for your answer.

16.

Would you rather be a dog or a cat? Write the reasons for your choice.

17.

Would you like to live to be 100 years old? Explain your answer.

18.

If you could be a superstar in any sport when you grow up, what sport would you choose? Explain your answer.

19.

Who or what makes you laugh? Explain why you think this person or thing is funny.

20.

Imagine that you drank a magic potion, and then suddenly you started to grow smaller and smaller. Finally, you were no larger than a fly. What would you do?

21.

If you had X-ray vision, what would you use it for?

22.

If you were a car, what name would you give yourself? Explain your choice.

23.

In the future, you might be able to take pills instead of eating meals. Explain why you would like or dislike taking these pills. For example, which foods would you like to take in pill form and which foods would you not like to take in pill form?

24.

Imagine that all television stations stopped broadcasting for one week. What would you do instead of watching TV that week?

25.

What is your most prized possession? Explain why it is so important to you.

26.

What do you think would happen to you if all of the clocks and watches in the world suddenly started to go back-wards?

27.

What makes you special or unique?

28.

Do you think that competitive sports like Little League baseball are or are not helpful to students in elementary school? Explain your answer.

29.

Based on what you now know about yourself, make five predictions about your future.

30.

Write about your favorite hobby. How did you get started? What do you like about it? Would you recommend it to others? (If you don't have a hobby, write about the hobby you would most like to have or explain why you are not inter-ested in having a hobby.)

31.

What do you like most about yourself? What do you like least about yourself? Explain your answers.

32.

What game or toy would you like to have that you don't have? Explain your choice.

33.

Imagine that you found an old trunk in your grandparents' attic. What would you like to find in the trunk? Explain the reasons for your choices.

34.

Explain the advantages and disadvantages of being able to fly around like a bird.

35.

If you could have any kind of animal as a pet, what would it be? Explain how you would take care of it, and tell how your parents would react to your having this animal as a pet.

36.

What do you like most about living in your town or city? What do you like least about it? Explain your answers.

37.

If you could plan your next birthday party, what would you do?

38.

Have you ever been lost? Explain what happened and how you felt then, and afterwards.

39.

What's the worst part about being sick? Explain your answer.

40.

Do you think you have a lot of self-confidence? Explain the reasons for your answer.

41.

What is the hardest decision you have ever had to make? Looking back on your decision, do you now think you made the right choice? Explain your answer.

42.

What is one goal or hope you have for the future? Explain why it is so important to you.

43.

How would you feel if there was a new law forbidding the playing of any music?

44.

Do you think you're shy? What advice could you give to someone who is shy?

45.

Write about a superstition you believe in. Explain why you believe in it.

46.

Who is a hero of yours? Explain why that person means so much to you.

47.

Imagine you have just been given the name and address of a pen pal. Write about yourself to that person.

48.
Explain why you would or would not like to get married some day.

49.
Retell a compliment that someone recently paid you. Explain how that compliment made you feel.

50.
Retell a compliment that you recently paid to someone else. Explain how you think your compliment made the other person feel.

51.
Explain how you think your life would be different if you had to be in a wheelchair.

52.
If you could be someone else, who would that person be? Explain your choice.

53.
List the three most important people you know. Then explain why these people are important (or important to you).

54.
Write some sayings for fortune cookies that you would like to get yourself.

55.
Explain what the word *prejudice* means to you. Then decide whether or not you think you're prejudiced.

56.
Which would you rather be: a fish or a bird? Explain your answer.

57.
Picture yourself ten years from now. Then write down any thoughts, ideas, or mental pictures of yourself that flash across your mind.

58.
Invent a new game or a new toy you think people your age would like.

59.
If this were January 1, what New Year's resolutions would you make?

60.
Explain why you do or not like to talk on the telephone.

61.
Imagine that you had to go to a deserted island for a week. In addition to food, shelter, and other necessities that will be provided, you are allowed to take three personal items. What would they be? Explain the reasons for your choices.

62.

Write about the thoughts and feelings you have when you listen to your favorite song.

63.

Invent something that would make doing homework easier.

64.

Explain why you think you are or are not a good loser.

65.

Make a timeline of the next twenty years of your life. List all the things that you would like to have happen in your life during those years.

66.

What would you do if you woke up at night to find that your room was filled with smoke?

67.

Would you prefer to live in a cold climate like Alaska's or a hot climate like Florida's? Explain the reasons for your choice.

68.

If you could be anything you want to be when you graduate from school, what would you be? Explain your choice.

70.

What is your favorite sport? Write the reasons for your choice. (If you don't have a favorite sport, decide what sport you would like to play well when you get older. Then list the reasons for your choice.)

71.

Write a short fairy tale in which you are a character. Begin with the words, "Once upon a time...."

72.

Invent the best dessert in the whole world.

73.

What season of the year do you like best? Write the reasons for your choice.

74.

Explain what you think is the meaning of the saying, "Beauty is only skin deep."

75.

Is there anything you want so much that you would be willing to save all of your own money to get? Explain your answer.

Chapter 2

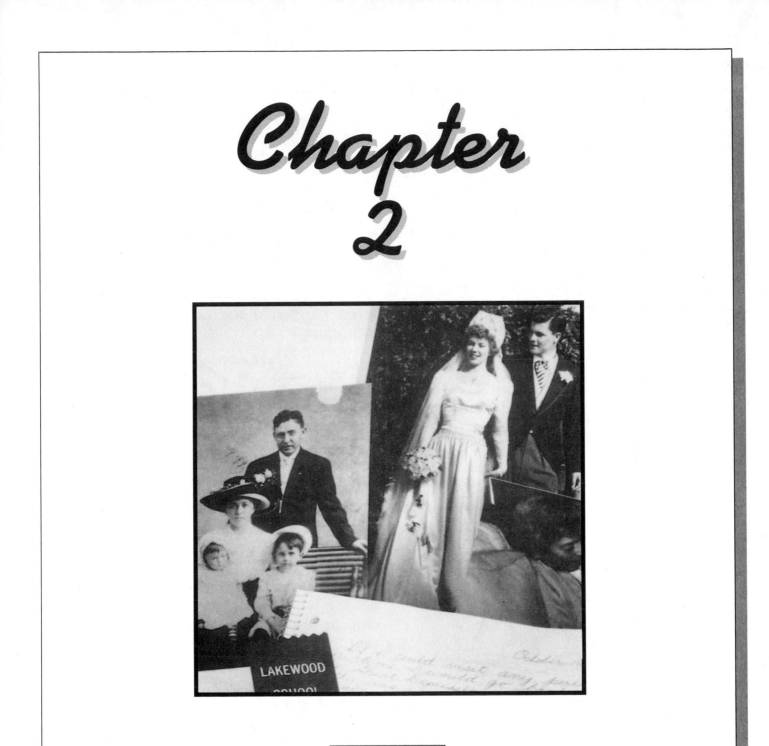

Memories

*E*qually important as present interests to young people are their past memories and experiences. These memories and experiences, after all, have contributed to making them who they are today—whether or not they realize that at the moment. Therefore, remembering, or reliving, some "first" experiences or recalling a former friend or teacher can open the floodgates of sensory experiences—the kind that can later be turned into colorful and exciting writing.

76.

Think of a photograph of yourself taken when you were younger. Then write down the thoughts that you might have been thinking at the time it was taken. (NOTE: Some students may want to include the actual photograph in their journals.)

77.

What is the funniest thing that has ever happened to you? Retell the event as completely as you can.

78.

Write about a "first" in your life—such as the first time you stayed home alone or the first time you stayed overnight at a friend's house.

79.

When you were younger, what was your favorite bedtime story? Explain why you liked it so much.

80.

What has been your favorite birthday present of all those you've received? Write the reasons for your answer.

81.

What is your earliest memory? Write as many details about it as you can recall.

82.

What did you like best about visiting a fair or an amusement park?

83.

What is the greatest thrill you have ever had in your life? Retell your experience in as much detail as possible.

84.

What happened the first time you went swimming?

85.

Make a timeline of your life—listing only the most important events that have happened so far.

86.

Write about a club or organization you belong to. Explain what you do in the club or organization and why it's important to you.

87.

What was the best thing that happened to you yesterday?

88.

What was the hardest thing for you to learn when you were very young? For example, you might have had trouble learning to tie your shoelaces or drinking from a straw. Explain how you finally learned to do it.

89.

Recall as clearly as possible an unusual dream that you've had.

90.

Write any memories, feelings, and/or happenings that come into your mind when you hear the word *fireworks*.

91.

What's the best idea you have ever had?

92.

Recall the last time you were scared or got "butterflies in your stomach."

93.

What do you think is your greatest accomplishment or achievement so far? Explain your answer.

94.

Write about a game or a toy you liked when you were very young. Explain why you liked it so much.

95.

Describe the best Halloween costume you have ever worn (or seen).

96.

Write about what you have done on a recent Saturday that you really enjoyed.

97.

Recall a time when you were a very good friend or a helper to someone else.

98.

If you could go back in time and do one thing differently, what would it be? Explain your answer.

99.

What is the one thing you remember most clearly about kindergarten or first grade? Explain why you think that memory is so clear.

100.

What is your earliest memory of your mother? Recall it with as much detail as possible.

101.

What is your earliest memory of your father? Recall it with as much detail as possible.

102.

Write about your first pet. Include a special memory about it. (If you have never had a pet, write about the kind of pet you would like to have one day.)

103.

What is your favorite ride at an amusement park? Explain your answer.

104.

Where did you go on your most favorite trip or vacation? Recall one special memory about that time.

105.

Recall a time when you learned how to do something—like ride a bicycle or hit a baseball.

106.

What is the biggest surprise you have

ever had in your life? Recall it with as much detail as possible.

107.

Write about the most beautiful or unusual bird or animal you have ever seen. What made it so special or unique?

108.

Explain what you have done in your life to deserve a medal.

109.

Write about the first meal you ever made for your family or friends. What was it? Did you have any problems making it? How did your family or friends like it?

110.

Recall the last time you were bored. Describe the situation and explain what you did about it.

111.

"When the cat's away, the mice will play" is an old proverb. Give one example of how this proverb has been true in your life.

112.

What was the most interesting name you ever gave to a pet? Explain how you came up with that name. (If you have never had a pet, make up some names for a pet you may have some time in the future.)

113.

Write about an object that you keep to remind you of someone or something. What is it? What memories does it bring back?

114.

Recall a time when you were in a play or had to give a speech in front of the class. What happened? How did you feel?

115.

Write about a race or some other competition you have been in.

Chapter 3

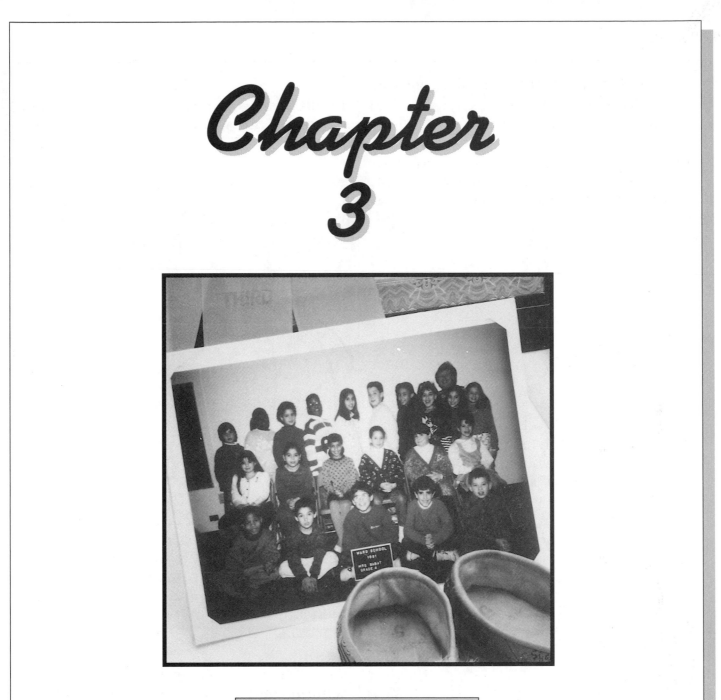

Families and Friends

If you ask your students to list the most important people in their lives, the majority would undoubtedly start with the names of family members and friends. These are the people who most directly influence them and affect changes in their lives, and it is this very interaction that provides the realistic basis for characters that they will write about throughout the school year. Therefore, when your students write in response to prompts in this chapter, remind them to write with as much description and detail as possible.

116.

Write down your ideas of what an ideal brother or sister would be like.

117.

Make a list of the advantages and disadvantages of being an only child.

118.

Who is your best friend? Explain the reasons why you like that person so much.

119.

What advice would you give to a younger brother or sister?

120.

Write a description of a family member. Include not only what that person looks like but also what kind of person he or she is.

121.

What's the nicest thing your best friend has ever done for you?

122.

What's the nicest thing you have ever done for your best friend?

123.

Recall as much as possible about your very first best friend.

124.

Write down your ideas of what a perfect parent would be—one you would like to be when you grow up, perhaps.

125.

Brainstorm a list of things you would like to do next summer with your family.

126.

If you were your best friend's fairy godmother, what would you do for him or her?

127.

Describe a recent photograph of your family. Explain why you were all together and why the picture was taken. (NOTE: Some students may also want to include the actual photograph in their journals.)

128.

What do you enjoy doing most with your best friend? Explain the reasons for your answer.

129.

What is it that makes you most angry at a brother or sister (or friend)? Explain your answer.

130.

Write about your favorite family tradition. What is it? How did it get started? How do you feel about it?

131.

Recall as much as possible about how you met your best friend.

132.

If you could become a different member of your family, who would you be? Explain your choice.

133.

What family duty or chore do you have that you like the least? Explain your answer.

134.

What are the most important qualities you look for in a friend?

135.

Write about a time when a family member or a friend embarrassed you. Then describe how you reacted. Looking back on that situation, do you feel any different about that experience now?

136.

Write about a major change that has occurred in your family recently—such as a move, a divorce, or a new member. Then explain what effect that change has had on you.

137.

Recall an interesting conversation you have recently had with a family member.

138.

Who is your favorite relative? Explain the reasons for your choice.

139.

What do you admire most about one of your grandparents (or other relative)? Explain the reasons for your answer.

140.

If you could be related to someone famous, who would that person be? Explain your choice.

141.

How do you think you could be a better friend?

142.

Recall a special time you have spent with one of your grandparents.

143.

If you were a parent, how would you get your children to do something they didn't want to do—like eat their vegetables or clean their room?

144.

Recall a time when a family member was able to change your mind about something.

145.

Write about a disagreement you have had with a brother or sister (or other family member). Then explain how that disagreement was resolved.

146.

"Parents have eyes in the back of their heads." Explain what you think this statement means, and whether you agree. If possible, give some actual examples to support your answer.

147.

If there were three children in your family, which one would you want to be: the oldest, the middle one, or the youngest one? Explain your choice.

148.

What would you like to give your mother (or father) for her (or his) next birthday? Write the reasons for your choice.

150.

Recall a time when something interesting or unusual happened when a babysitter was in charge.

151.

Norma Simon wrote, "A family is people who belong together." Explain how your family belongs together.

152.

What have you ever learned from a grandparent (or other older person)?

153.

What would you do if you wanted to meet your friends, but your mother said you had to take your younger brother or sister along with you?

154.

If you had a suggestion box at your home, what suggestions would you make?

155.

Write about the kind of parent you think you will be.

156.

Among the members of your family, who understands you the best? Explain your answer.

157.

If you were planning a movie about your family, what title would you give it? Explain your answer.

158.

What do you do that helps a family member (or a friend) the most? Explain your answer.

159.

If your best friends started to smoke or use drugs, would you? Explain the reasons why you would or would not join them.

160.

What is one subject you would like to be able to talk to your parents about? Explain why you think you can't discuss this subject with them.

Chapter 4

Current Affairs

*I*n what areas are most of your students experts? Answers would surely include the newest video games, the hottest television shows, the top songs on MTV, and the latest clothing fads. These types of "current affairs" are very important to young people because they help to identify who they are, and they provide a comfortable haven of familiarity and conformity. By having your students write about the various "current affairs" in their lives, you will be sending out a message that you understand how important these things are to them and, therefore, to their writing.

161.

What is a current fad? Explain why you do or do not like it.

162.

Explain a time when an advertisement or a commercial made you want to buy something.

163.

List ways your life would be different if you could never again use a telephone.

164.

Explain why you think using a computer could help you become a better student.

165.

What are some ways you could make your pet's life better? (If you don't have a pet, think of ways you would make your pet's life better if you had one.)

166.

What would you do with a million dollars?

167.

Write about typical teenagers today. What do they look like? (NOTE: Some students may prefer to draw a picture first.) What do they like to do? What are their likes and dislikes?

168.

Why do you watch movies or TV shows that you know will scare you?

169.

Explain why you like or don't like to read comic books.

170.

If you were going to write to one famous person, who would that person be? What would you say in your letter?

171.

Do you believe in superstitions? Explain your answer.

172.

Why do you think almost everyone loves Charlie Brown and Snoopy?

173.

If you could give the President of the United States one piece of advice, what would it be? Explain your answer.

174.

What is your favorite cartoon or comic strip? Explain the reasons for your choice.

175.

What do you think is the hardest choice young people your age have to make?

176.

What do you collect—such as stickers, baseball cards, rocks? Explain why you started your collection. (If you don't collect anything, describe what you would like to collect or explain why you don't like to collect things.)

177.

What is your favorite TV show? Write the reasons for your choice.

178.

What do you think is good about television?

179.

What do you think is bad about television?

180.

Why do you think so many young people watch MTV?

181.

How much television do you watch a week? Do you think you watch too much television? Explain your answer.

182.

Write down a joke that you know. Then try to make up one yourself.

183.

Write a brief summary of a book you have read recently. Then explain why you did or did not like it.

184.

If you could star in your own TV show, what would that show be about? Explain the reasons for your choice.

185.

Space exploration costs billions of dollars. Do you think this money is being spent wisely or foolishly? For example, do you think there is any way that space exploration could ever directly affect your life?

186.

Write about your first airplane ride. (If you have never been on an airplane, describe what you think it would be like.)

187.

What is your favorite kind of car? Explain why you think cars are so important to Americans.

188.

List the things or people that make you sad or make you feel bad.

189.

List the things or people that make you happy or make you feel good.

190.

How do you feel about young people who use drugs?

191.

Explain why you do or do not like to play video games.

192.

List the qualifications you have for some kind of a job—such as delivering the newspaper or babysitting.

193.

Do you think life is harder for a girl or a boy? Or, do you think there's no difference at all? Explain your answer.

194.

Imagine that you and your friends all like a particular fad, but your parents don't approve of it. How would you try to resolve this problem?

195.

What is the best movie that you have seen in the past year? Explain your choice.

196.

How do you think the divorce of parents affects the lives of their children?

197.

What issue or story in the news concerns you the most? Explain your answer.

198.

What do you think makes some students so popular with their classmates?

199.

List the reasons why you think people get divorced.

200.

What have you learned about eating healthy foods in the past couple of years? Do you ever eat foods you know are not healthy? If so, explain why.

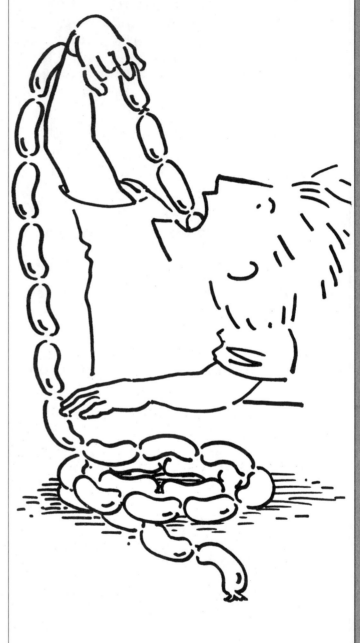

Chapter 5

School Subjects

The topics in this chapter are valuable for two main reasons. First, because a large part of your students' lives revolves around school; they need to think about it and write about it. Second, they will help you make the point repeatedly throughout the year that writing is important in all school subjects; its relevance is not limited merely to language arts. This application of your students' writing skills to other subject areas is a life-long lesson of the greatest significance.

201.
If you were a fish and could talk, what would you say to humans?

202.
If you could visit any place in the world for the first time, where would you go? Write the reasons for your answer.

203.
What is your favorite subject in school? Explain why you like it.

204.
Explain why you like or dislike riding on a school bus. (If you don't ride on a school bus, explain why it would or would not be preferable to whatever means you presently take to school.)

205.
Would you like to be an astronaut on the first mission to an unexplored planet or a new galaxy? Explain your answer.

206.
Imagine that you had a chance to talk to a cave man. List the questions you would like to ask.

207.
Write everything that comes to your mind when you hear the words *endangered species.*

208.
Write about the best teacher you have ever had. What made that teacher so special?

209.
What would you like to learn about in school that you don't know about now?

210.
Explain ways in which the weather has some direct effect on your life.

211.
When you see a picture of the Statue of Liberty, what thoughts go through your mind? Do you think statues like the Statue of Liberty are important?

212.
If you were the principal of your school, what would you do to make the school better?

213.
What do you think you could learn from a butterfly?

214.
How do you think your life would be different if the Declaration of Independence had never been written and signed?

215.
List the ways that you could help to improve the environment in your neighborhood or community.

216.

Do you think that recycling is important or just a waste of time?

217.

Would you like to be President of the United States when you grow up? Explain the reasons for your answer.

218.

Imagine that you are an animal in a zoo. Write what thoughts and feelings you might have.

219.

Explain why you think creatures do or do not exist on other planets or in other galaxies.

220.

If you could write several new rules for your school, what would they be? Explain why your new rules are fair, and should be obeyed.

221.

List the ways you think you can avoid catching a cold.

222.

Brainstorm a good slogan for the next Earth Day—one that has some special meaning to you.

223.

What things would you put into a time capsule today that would tell people living a thousand years from now something about people today? Write the reasons for your choices.

224.

What instrument would you most like to play in the school band? Explain your answer. (If you already play an instrument, explain why you chose that instrument.)

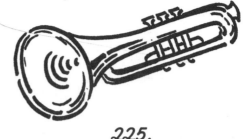

225.

If you could travel through time, what period in the past or the future would you like to visit? Explain your choice.

226.

Do you think smoking should be against the law, or should people have the right to smoke—even if it hurts their health or the health of those around them?

227.

Explain why you do or do not believe in UFO's.

228.

Create a never-before-discovered bird or animal. After you describe how it looks, tell more about it—such as what unusual things it can do, what it eats, and what kinds of sounds it makes.

229.

What explorer—such as Christopher Columbus, Marco Polo, or Lewis and Clark—would you have liked to travel with the most? Explain your answer.

230.

Why do you think no woman has ever been elected President of the United States? How long do you think it will be before a woman is elected President? Do you think a woman will govern differently from a man? Explain the reasons for your answers.

231.

What are some reasons why understanding math could be helpful in your future life?

232.

Write about a time when you tried to teach someone else how to do something; for example, you might have tried to teach a younger brother or sister how to rollerskate.

233.

How would you improve the food in your school's cafeteria?

234.

Do you think students should or should not wear uniforms to school? Explain your answer.

235.

Invent a school of the future—one that you would like to attend. How would it be different from your school now? How would it be the same?

236.

Do you think a school is the only place you can get an education? Explain your answer.

237.

Explain how you might feel if you were German and had seen the Berlin Wall come down.

238.

What is the best part of the school day for you? Explain your answer.

239.

Explain why you do or do not like to give a speech in front of your class.

240.

If you could be a friend of any one of the Presidents of the United States—past or present—whom would you choose? Explain the reasons for your choice.

241.

Explain why you do or do not like math.

242.

Explain how you come up with ideas to write about.

243.

Write about what you think your life would be like as an adult if you had never learned to read.

244.

Explain why you do or do not believe in creatures like the Loch Ness monster and Bigfoot.

245.

If you could create a robot that could do anything, what would you want it to do? Explain your answer.

Chapter 6

Multicultural Connections

In recent years many educators have begun to realize that students' unique backgrounds and cultural heritages are important topics to read about, talk about, and write about. Equally important for students is the exercise of trying to see through the eyes of those who have different cultural backgrounds and heritages. The prompts in this chapter will help your students write about what they know about themselves and their ancestors, and how they feel about others.

246.

Write several questions you would like to ask someone your age who lives in China. What questions do you think they'd like to ask you?

247.

What advice would you give to a new student from a foreign country?

248.

If you had a pen pal in South America, what would you want to ask that person about his or her life?

249.

Why do you think some people dislike other people—is it just because they look different?

250.

What country did one of your ancestors come from? Explain how you think your life would have been different if you were living in that country today.

251.

Explain why you would or would not ever listen to a song that is sung in a language that you do not understand.

252.

Write about a tradition that was started by an ancestor of yours and is still followed by your family today.

253.

Explain what you think the following Chinese proverb means: "With time and patience, the mulberry leaf becomes a silk gown."

254.

List the questions you would want to ask a girl from Japan who has just entered your class. For example, what would you like to know about her country, her background, and her traditions?

255.

What would you fear most about moving to another country?

256.

If you could live in another country for six months, what country would you choose? How do you think living there would be different from where you're living now?

257.

Why do you think that people with different ancestry or cultural backgrounds sometimes have problems getting along with each other?

258.

Imagine that you are a Native American. Write about the things that would trouble or concern you the most.

259.

Write about someone you know who grew up in a culture that is different from your own. What do you like about that person? What is different or unique about that person? What about them is similar to you?

260.

What are some general attitudes that Americans have toward people who live in Third World countries? Do you agree or disagree with them? Explain your answers.

261.

What holidays or celebrations are important to your family? Why? What do you and your family do on those days?

263.

What would you like to learn about the people who live in Australia?

264.

Write everything you know about your ancestors on your mother's side of the family.

265.

Write everything you know about your ancestors on your father's side of the family.

266.

What do you think people in other countries think of America and the American people? What do you think would be the biggest surprise an immigrant to the United States would have?

267.

Write freely about what you think the following Native American proverb means: "Never criticize a man until you've walked a mile in his moccasins."

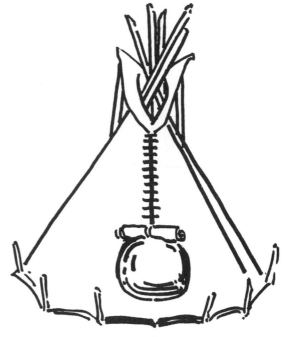

268

If you could learn one foreign language, which one would you choose? Explain your answer.

269.

What makes you most proud to be an American?

270.

What could you learn from a friend or classmate who is from another country?

271.

What could you teach a friend or classmate who is from another country?

272.

Write whatever comes into your mind when you read the following Spanish proverb: "Three helping one another will do as much as six men singly."

273.

Japanese Zen masters teach people to look for beauty in everyday things. Look around to find an ordinary object, and then look closely to find something beautiful in it. Explain what it is and why you think you never saw how beautiful it was before.

274.

What are some foods you and your family eat that reflect your cultural background?

275.

Explain what you think it would be like to move to a country where you couldn't speak the language or understand a single word.

276.

Recall everything you know about your first and last names—such as their origin and meaning.

277.

What country—other than your own—do you most admire? Write the reasons for your choice.

278.

If you lived in another country, why might you want to immigrate to the United States?

279.

Write what you think the following Ethiopian proverb means: "When spider webs unite, they can tie up a lion."

280.

What is one object or symbol that is important to your cultural background?

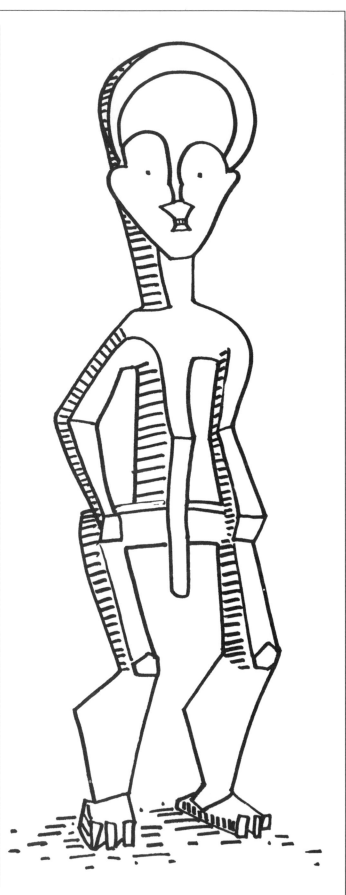

Chapter 7

Quotations

The prompts in this chapter cover many different topics and areas because they spring from quotations by some famous and not-so-famous people and fictional characters. Sometimes students are asked to react to what someone has said, and at other times they are asked to explain what they think the speaker or writer meant by a certain quotation. The object of these prompts, however, is simply to write about a topic of personal relevance; it's not to write about literature. The option is open to you, nevertheless, to read these quotations to your students within the context of the entire piece of literature from which they were taken.

281.

A familiar nursery rhyme begins:
  "Twinkle, twinkle, little star,
  How I wonder what you are!
  Up above the world so high,
  Like a diamond in the sky"

List everything that is valuable or precious to you, and tell why you value it .

282.

In "Horton Hatches the Egg," by Dr. Seuss, Horton the elephant says,
  "I meant what I said
  And I said what I meant....
  An elephant's faithful
  One hundred percent!"

What do you think Horton meant when he said this?

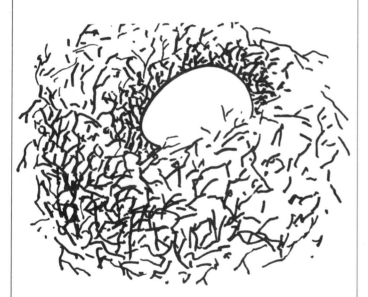

283.

In the poem "If I Were King" by A.A. Milne, Christopher Robin says,
  "I often wish I were a King,
  And then I could do anything."

What are some things you would do if you became the king of your own country? Do you think there might be some things you could not do, precisely because you were king? Explain your answers.

284.

In "The Tale of Tom Kitten" by Beatrix Potter, Mrs. Tabitha Twitchit says to her three kittens, "Now keep your frocks clean, children! You must walk on your hind legs. Keep away from the dirty ash-pit, and from Sally Henny Penny, and from the pig-stye, and the Puddle-ducks."

What is some advice your mother has given you? How do you feel when you receive advice? Even if it is for your own good, do you sometimes hate to hear it? Or do you appreciate it? Explain your answer.

285.

In the story "Raggedy Ann Learns a Lesson" by Johnny Gruelle, Raggedy Ann tells the other dolls, "And our lesson was that we must never take without asking what we could always have for the asking!"

What do you think Raggedy Ann meant?

286.

In the poem "Happy Thought," Robert Louis Stevenson says,
  "The world is so full of a number of things,
  I'm sure we should all be as happy as kings."

List all of the things that make you happy.

287.

In the story "Beauty and the Beast" by Walter Crane, Beast asks Beauty,

"Am I so very ugly?" Beauty replied, "Yes, indeed you are, but then you are so kind that I don't mind your looks."

Explain what you can learn from Beauty.

288.

Robert Louis Stevenson begins the poem "The Little Land,"

"When at home alone I sit,
And am very tired of it,
I have just to shut my eyes
To go sailing through the skies—"

Write about your most common day-dream.

289.

The last words in the story "The Lorax" by Dr. Seuss are:

"UNLESS someone like you
cares a whole awful lot,
nothing is going to get better.
It's not."

What do those words mean to you?

290.

One of Winnie-the-Pooh's songs by A. A. Milne goes like this:

"Isn't it funny
How a bear likes honey?
Buzz! Buzz! Buzz!
I wonder why he does?"

List all of the foods you like to eat. Can you write a poem or song about your favorite food, they way Winnie-the-Pooh does?

291.

When the Genie in the lamp appeared to Aladdin, he asked, "What wouldest thou have? I am ready to obey thee as thy slave...."

If you could have one wish, what would it be? Explain your answer.

292.

In "The Adventures of Peter Cottontail" by Thornton W. Burgess, Peter Rabbit says, "Cottontail, Peter Cottontail! How much better sounding that is than Peter Rabbit! That sounds as if I were really somebody. Yes, Sir, that's the very name I want."

If you could change your name, what would it be? Explain your answer.

293.

An old nursery rhyme begins, "Little Bo-Peep has lost her sheep, and can't tell where to find them;"

Write about something that you once lost and explain how you found it.

294.

"The Story of Babar" by Jean De Brunhoff ends with these words: "And now King Babar and Queen Celeste, both eager for further adventures, set out on their honeymoon in a gorgeous yellow balloon."

If you could set out on an adventure tomorrow, where would you go and how would you get there? Explain your answers.

295.

In the story "The Velveteen Rabbit" by Margery Williams Bianco, the Skin Horse says to the velveteen Rabbit, "When a child loves you for a long, long time, not just to play with, but REALLY loves you, then you become Real."

Write about the one toy you have had at any time in your life that you have loved the most.

296.

The story "Puss in Boots" by Charles Perrault ends with these words: "Puss became a great lord and gave up chasing mice except just once in a while for the fun of it."

List the things that you like to do "just for the fun of it."

297.

At the end of "The Tale of Johnny Town-Mouse, "Beatrix Potter wrote: "One place suits one person, another place suits another person."

What kind of place suits you more? Explain your answer.

298.

In the "The Wind in the Willows" by Kenneth Grahame, Mole says, "Toad's hour, of course!...I remember now! We'll teach him to be a sensible Toad!"

Do you think people can be taught to be sensible? Explain your answer.

299.

An old nursery rhyme begins, "Baa, baa, black sheep, have you any wool? Yes, sir, yes, sir, three bags full."

Write a conversation you would like to have with an animal.

300.

The following lines are from the poem "The Walrus and the Carpenter" by Lewis Carroll: "'The time has come,' the Walrus said, 'To talk of many things: Of shoes—and ships—and sealing wax—Of cabbages—and kings—'"

List all of your favorite things to talk about.

301.

In the poem "In the Fashion," A. A. Milne writes, "A lion has a tail and a very fine tail, And so has an elephant, and so has a whale, And so has a crocodile, and so has a quail— They've all got tails but me."

Explain what you think would be both the advantages and disadvantages of your having a tail.

302.

In *Charlotte's Web* by E. B. White, Mr. Zuckerman says, "A miracle has happened on this farm."

Write about the closest thing to a miracle that you have ever seen or heard about.

303.

In "Snow White and the Seven Dwarfs" by the Brothers Grimm, the Queen asks her magic mirror,
"Magic mirror on the wall, Who is the fairest of us all?"

What does the Queen mean by "fairest"? (NOTE: students may not know that "fair" in this usage means "pretty".) Who is "the fairest" person you know? Write about that person.

304.

Miss Piggy once advised, "Never eat more than you can lift."

What is some advice about eating, or anything else, you could give to your friends?

305.

The moral of Aesop's fable "The Fox and the Goat" is "Look before you leap."

What do you think this moral means?

306.

In *Through the Looking Glass* by Lewis Carroll, Alice laughed and said, "There's no use trying, one can't believe impossible things."

Explain why you agree or disagree with Alice.

307.

In the play *I Remember Mama* by John van Druten, the mother tells her daughter, "I would like to be rich the way I would like to be ten feet high. [It] would be good for some things—bad for others."

Write about some disadvantages of being rich.

308.

Speaking to a group of parents, Jesse Jackson once said, "Your children need your presence more than your presents."

What do you think he meant?

309.

William Durant, the founder of General Motors, once said, "Forget mistakes. Forget failures. Forget everything except what you're going to do today. Today is your lucky day."

Write about how today is your lucky day.

310.

In the play "The Glass Menagerie" by Tennessee Williams, Jim knocks over a glass unicorn that belongs to Laura. Then she says, "Now he's just like all the other horses....He's lost his horn. It doesn't matter. Maybe it's a blessing in disguise."

What do you think Laura means by a "blessing in disguise"? Has anything ever happened to you that turned out to be a "blessing in disguise?" Explain.

311.

Dr. Karl Menninger once wrote, "Fears are educated into us, and can, if we wish, be educated out."

Explain what you think he meant.

312.

Dr. Joyce Brothers once said, "When you look at your life, the greatest happinesses are family happinesses."

Recall one of the happiest moments your family has ever had together.

313.

In the book *Rascal* by Sterling North, the teacher tells the class about raccoons. "As you can see," she said, "raccoons are curious."

List the things that you are most curious about.

314.

In *Poor Richard's Almanack*, Benjamin Franklin wrote, "Don't throw stones at your neighbours', if your own Windows are glass."

What do you think he meant?

315.

In the book *Superfudge* by Judy Blume, the principal tells Fudge, "But we do have rules here....and you will have to obey them"

What are some rules at school or at home that you have to obey?

316.

Nancy Thayer once wrote, "It's never too late—in fiction or in life—to revise."

Explain at least one thing you would "revise," or change, in your life.

317.

The great architect Frank Lloyd Wright once said, "Television is chewing gum for the eyes."

What do you think he meant?

318.

Anne Frank wrote in her diary, "I don't think of all the misery, but of all the beauty that still remains." (NOTE: stu-

dents may not be familiar with Anne Frank, or with the Holocaust. This prompt may best be used after a discussion of the events of World War II.)

List the things you think are the most beautiful in your life. Do beautiful things help you to forget some of life's "misery"? Explain.

319.

The following words are from the song "Home, Sweet Home" by John Howard Payne: "Be it ever so humble, there's no place like home."

Explain what you like the most about your home.

320.

The following statement was from the 1972 Only One Earth Conference: "We have forgotten how to be good guests, how to walk lightly on the earth as other creatures do."

What do you think this statement means?

321.

The Pledge of Allegiance says, "I pledge allegiance to the flag of the United States of America, and to the Republic for which it stands, one nation under God, indivisible, with liberty and justice for all."

What do these words mean to you?

322.

A man by the name of George Santayana once said, "A child educated only at school is an uneducated child."

What do you think he meant?

323.

Anäis Nin once said, "What I cannot love, I overlook. Is that real friendship?"

What answer would you give to her?

324.

Chief Seattle wrote, "We are part of the earth and it is part of us.The perfumed flowers are our sisters. The bear, the deer, and the great eagle, these are our brothers...."

What do you think he meant by this?

325.

In John F. Kennedy's inaugural address, he said, "And so, my fellow Americans: Ask not what your country can do for you—ask what you can do for your country."

What do you think you can do for your country, now and in the future?

Bibliography

Dionisio, Marie.
**"Responding to Literary Elements through
Mini-lessons and Dialogue Journals."**
English Journal, January 1991: 38-44.

Latta, Dawn.
**"In-Process and Retrospective Journals:
Putting Writers Back in Writing Processes."**
English Journal, January 1991: 60-66.

Sullivan, Anne McCrary.
**"Liberating the Urge to Write: From Classroom
Journals to Lifelong Writing."**
English Journal, November 1989: 55-61.

Wollman-Bonilla, Julie.
Response Journals
New York: Scholastic, Inc., 1991.

Schall, Jane.
Write Every Day.
New York: Scholastic, Inc., 1990.